CHRISTIAN V
The First Heir
to the Throne

by Jens Gunni Busck

Historika

Published in cooperation with the Royal Danish Collection

CONTENTS

Detail of Christian V's crown. His monogram in gold thread can be seen under the rectangular stone over the large sapphire.

　Christian V – The First Heir to the Throne

A HEREDITARY KING'S CHALLENGES

In 1670, Christian V succeeded Frederik III, who had introduced a hereditary and absolute monarchy in Denmark. Christian V was thus the first successor who automatically became King the moment his father died. He inherited a young and untested political system in which the power of the King was theoretically unlimited, but the manner in which power was in fact to be administered was largely an unresolved question. Christian V's big challenge would be to find his footing as the man at the centre of the absolutist state and secure its existence for the future. And not least he inherited an account to settle with Denmark's main enemy, Sweden.

Portrait of Christian V, attributed to Abraham Wuchters.

The absolute monarchy was only ten years old when Christian V became King. The old nobility hoped that he would be a less headstrong ruler than his father had been and prove to be more pliable in his relationship with that once so powerful class, but they were disappointed. Christian V felt that he had an obligation to manage the legacy of his father, and while he had not inherited all of Frederik III's wisdom and far-sightedness, he oversaw significant consolidation and further development of the absolutist state during the decades that followed. When he died in 1699, he left behind a system that was much more well-established than the one he had inherited himself.

He was less successful, however, in his attempts to reconquer the territories—including Scania, Halland, and Blekinge—which had been lost to Sweden in connection with the Treaty of Roskilde in 1658. The Scanian War, which lasted from 1675 to 1679, was entangled with a major European war, and when France, a great power, dictated a peace treaty between Denmark and Sweden, Christian V was not permitted to keep any of the territory he had won at all. This lack of military success is probably an important reason why Christian V is not one of the best-remembered of the Danish kings.

However, there is no doubt that Christian V is among the more likeable kings in Danish history. He actually had a hard time saying no to people, and this meant that he faced some particular challenges as a king. The absolute monarchy meant that the court became the only political arena of the age, one in which people fought for the favour of the King, so Christian V had to learn to be at the centre of everyone's attention and simultaneously keep the right people in his vicinity and keep others at arm's length. The apparatus of the state demanded a well-defined hierarchy, and the King was dependent upon having loyal officials. Competition among these officials was fierce, and a series of influential advisors left their mark on Christian V's time as King. These included Peter Griffenfeld, who dominated the court for a few years as First Minister until the King found it necessary to get rid of him.

In a way, the state is the main character of Christian V's story because the state underwent great changes during his reign. A new social hierarchy was built up in which state finances were increasingly based on an explosively growing tax burden, the state was radically militarised, and the laws of the realm were codified and adjusted to the new model of government. In the midst of this machinery stood a good-natured and fairly uncomplicated fellow who was really happiest enjoying outdoor life and informal social activities but was required to fulfil his destiny as one of Europe's most sovereign rulers.

Claiming the inheritance

Prince Christian V was born in Flensburg on 15 April 1646. He was the first child to result from the marriage of Duke Frederik (III) and Sophie Amalie of Brunswick-Lüneburg. At the time of his birth, it did not appear particularly likely that the prince would become King, as "the Chosen" Prince Christian (Duke Frederik's elder brother) was positioned to succeed Christian IV to the throne of Denmark. Duke Frederik had lost his prince-bishoprics in Northern Germany as a result of the Torstenson War and was now Governor of the duchies, but the family's prospects for the future changed when the Chosen Prince died the following year. Duke Frederik now succeeded Christian IV as King of Denmark, and because Denmark-Norway was still an electoral monarchy when he acceded to the throne, he had to sign a håndfæstning (a contract regarding the conditions and limitations that would apply to his rule) that made the rigsråd (Council of the Realm), an assembly of noblemen, stronger than ever.

Prince Christian as portrayed by Karel van Mander as a newly chosen successor to the throne in 1650. The four-year-old boy is splendidly dressed and surrounded by objects associated with military endeavours. The portrait provides a certain sense of the prince's early education and of the self-understanding of the monarchy. At this point in time, it was considered clear that the Torstenson War (1643–45) had not been the final accounting with Sweden.

Enamel portrait of Frederik III's five eldest children, executed by Paul Prieur in 1671 after a painting from 1652 that was subsequently lost. Prince Christian is shown self-confidently drawing his bow as his younger sisters watch admiringly.

In 1651, little Prince Christian was hailed by representatives of the estates of the realm as his father's successor, though it was expected that he, too, would sign a håndfæstning when the time came. With this his future was certain, and the prince was thoroughly schooled with a view to preparing him to face his future tasks. He learned the necessary languages (Danish, German, and French) and displayed an aptitude for mathematics and music. The prince was also trained in the construction of fortifications, and this training was to stand him in good stead when he had become King. In contrast, it did not prove possible to awaken in him an interest in book-learning despite Frederik III's own strong attraction to such learning. The son instead took pleasure in physical activities, and he distinguished himself in knightly disciplines such as riding, fencing, and dancing. This would never change.

When the prince was fourteen years old, the transformation of the state occurred that would make him the first heir to the throne. This transformation had been preceded by several years of war with Sweden that had left Denmark suffering and ravaged, and this must have made a strong impression on the boy. However, it had proved possible to defend Copenhagen, which had survived a three-year siege, and because Frederik III and Sophie Amalie had remained in the city and had actively participated in its defence, the King enjoyed massive support in the capital after the war. In contrast, the nobility were to a great extent held responsible for the defeat, and it was in this context that the assembly of the estates of the realm of September 1660 led to the coup d'état that made Frederik III the first king of a hereditary line.

With the introduction of the hereditary monarchy, the high nobility lost their right to establish conditions by means of a håndfæstning that would limit the King's power, and this was in fact a revolutionary change. While it had been customary throughout the Middle Ages already for a king's eldest son to become the successor to the throne, the King nevertheless had to be elected, and he had to comply with the conditions that had been established in connection with the election. Now there was no longer a choice to be made, and on top of this, Frederik III was given free hands with regard to designing the political system that would be used from this point onwards. He exploited this freedom to introduce absolute monarchy, that is, a political system in which the power of the King is theoretically unlimited and not balanced by powerful groups of individuals such as the Council of the Realm or the assemblies of the classes. The introduction of hereditary and absolute monarchy meant that Prince Christian no longer had the status of an elected successor to the throne; rather, he was now a direct heir to the throne and therefore to absolute power.

Educational travel and marriage

Shortly after he had introduced absolute monarchy, Frederik III decided to send his son on a journey so he could establish international contacts and prepare for his com-

Christian V loved hunting more than any other pastime, and in France, he engaged in falcon hunting with falcons he had brought with him from Denmark. He may have used the equipment depicted here, which, like this still life by the Flemish painter C. N. Gijsbrecht, is kept at Rosenborg.

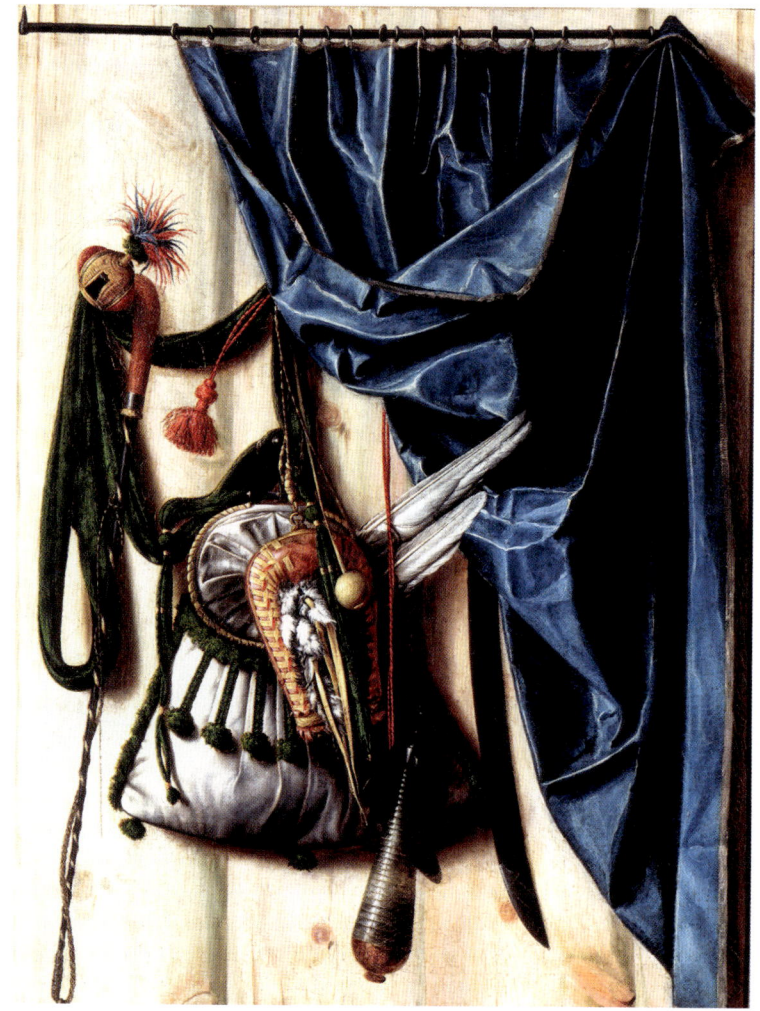

ing time as King. Prince Christian set forth early in the summer of 1662 with a retinue of fifteen persons, travelling first to the Netherlands, where he was happy to have the company of his half-brother Ulrik Frederik Gyldenløve, who was the son of Frederik III from Frederik's time as a prince-bishop and was eight years older than Prince Christian. The prince was travelling incognito, but when the company reached London after a brief

This 1768 map from the Royal Danish Academy of Sciences and Letters shows the clear traces left on the landscapes of North Zealand by Christian V's interest in hunting. He brought home from France the star-shaped systems of hunting paths that made it possible to maintain an overview of the hunt from a central position, and he combined such systems with the squares used in Saxony, while Jægersborg Dyrehave was dedicated to the freer English par force hunting. Christian V thus developed a very international system of par force hunting in the forests of North Zealand that is exceptionally well-preserved today. This hunting landscape was added to the UNESCO World Heritage list in 2015.

stop in Belgium (the Spanish Netherlands), it became more difficult to remain anonymous. At home in Copenhagen, the King received reports to the effect that the prince was enjoying his social life and neglecting his studies, and there were no fewer temptations in Paris, where the Danish successor's encounter with the splendid court of Louis XIV came as a revelation. The Sun King proved to be a very accommodating host, and

Queen Charlotte Amalie in a triumphal chariot. Engraved mother-of-pearl, inlaid in a slate tablet. Possibly executed by Jeremias Hercules. Fama (the Roman goddess of fame) holds a laurel wreath, while Mercury, the god of travellers, drives the chariot, which is pulled by elephants.

he involved his young guest in the life of the French court, which at this time was setting the international royal standard for magnificence and etiquette. Among other activities to which the Danish prince was introduced was par force hunting (a form of hunting in which one gets dogs to tire out the prey, after which the prey can be killed by a mounted hunter), which Louis XIV recommended that the prince import into Denmark. This laid the foundation of a lifelong passion, and the future King left Paris with a solid belief that absolute monarchy was the proper form of government.

A planned trip to Italy had to be given up to save money, but when the prince returned home after a year abroad, his parents expressed joy over positive changes. The years between Prince Christian's return to Denmark and his accession to the throne were undramatic, though a significant event did occur on 25 June 1667, when he married the seventeen-year-old princess Charlotte Amalie of Hesse-Kassel at the palace in Nykøbing Falster. She was a daughter of Landgrave William VI of Hesse-Kassel and Landgravine Hedwig Sophie, who was the sister of the "Great Electoral Prince" of Brandenburg and ruled the little state of Hesse-Kassel after her husband's death. Prince Christian had visited the family two years previously; probably he had been encouraged to do so by Queen Sophie Amalie. According to tradition, the Queen was interested in having a pliant daughter-in-law who would not be a serious contender to outshine the Queen herself if she became a dowager queen. One fact that speaks in favour of this interpretation is that there was an important reason why Sophie Amalie was a problematic choice. She was a Calvinist and determined to retain her faith, indeed making her ability to do so a precondition for the marriage. For their part, the Danish side required that any children resulting from the marriage would be raised in the Lutheran faith and that Charlotte Amalie would learn Danish, an undertaking in which she succeeded very well.

In general, the future queen turned out to have an excellent sense of and talent for the demanding social interactions at the court. Her own courtiers were mostly Reformed foreigners, but she was highly respected and was described remarkably positively in several reports written by foreign envoys. She was also a businesswoman, in fact quite a good one. Already while she was still Crown Princess, Frederik III transferred the estates Frederiksdal, Bagsværd, and Gentoftegård to her, and she later bought other estates in Stevns and Jutland and also established two paper mills. Above all, Charlotte Amalie fought tirelessly on behalf of the Reformed Church in Denmark, and every year representatives of that church still bring a bouquet to her sarcophagus in Roskilde Cathedral.

It remains a bit of a mystery why Frederik III did not involve his son in the running of the state to prepare him for taking on his inheritance. One reason could be that the relationship between Frederik III and his queen became downright inimical during the King's last years and that his son was under the influence of Sophie Amalie. There may also have been a certain distance between the father and son because the prince had truly inherited nothing of Frederik III's cool intellectualism. Whatever the reason, the prince was given almost no political responsibilities. Starting in 1664, he was allowed to attend negotiations of the government college, but it was not until shortly before his father's death that he was given a seat in the Privy Council (which had replaced the old Council of the Realm) and the Supreme Court.

Accession to the throne

Frederik III died on 9 February 1670 following a brief illness, and as has been mentioned, Christian V became King the moment his father expired—a principle that re-

View of Kongens Nytorv by J. J. Bruun, 1745. During his first years as King, Christian V, having been inspired by his time in France, had a place royale—a square in which instead of a market there is a central statue of a king—added to the Danish capital. Nyhavn (the "New Harbour") was excavated during the period 1671–73, while Kongens Nytorv was being created, and Ulrik Frederik Gyldenløve also built his palace during these years. After Christian V's death, the palace was named Charlottenborg. The King was also behind the construction of the low building in the background, which was a cannon foundry on the later site of the Royal Theatre. The equestrian statue of Christian V, which was originally of lead, was erected in 1688.

Christian V in conversation with his elder half-brother Ulrik Frederik Gyldenløve and Count Anthon of Aldenburg. This is a so-called grisaille (the word comes from the French gris, "grey") by Anton Steenwinkel; it was painted around 1671. Gyldenløverne, "the Golden Lions," were the King's "natural" children, that is, those of his children who had been conceived outside of his marriage, and they played an important role in the politics of the seventeenth century. They were excluded from potential succession to the throne and did not represent a threat to the reigning king in a dynastic sense, and for precisely this reason, they could be completely loyal to the King. Ulrik Frederik Gyldenløve (1638–1704) performed important

mains applicable today. While his predecessors had let themselves be hailed in public by the nobility and the other classes, Christian V simply accepted the oaths of fealty of the highest officials at the palace. Negotiations regarding a håndfæstning were no longer necessary, but as a kind of replacement, the new constitution of the absolute monarchy, the Royal Law, was ceremonially read aloud on 23 February.

With its fixed line of succession, the new system should actually have made a change of rulers easier, but the lack of an established tradition created uncertainty. The nobility had hopes of having some of their privileges reinstated, so many noblemen made a pilgrimage to the capital to advance their interests, but they soon discovered that absolute monarchy had come to stay.

In a system in which securing the King's favour was of decisive importance, however, a change of kings was a significant event for all influential individuals. There was no guarantee that having had a good relationship with the deceased King would ensure a good relationship with his successor, and the change of kings meant a restructuring of all the existing networks surrounding the monarch, a process that was bound to be associated with various manoeuvres and intrigues. Christoffer Gabel, who had previously been a very powerful individual, was soon negatively affected and had to resign his post, while Ulrik Frederik Gyldenløve (Christian V's half-brother and the Governor of Norway) and Frederik Ahlefeldt (the Governor of the duchies) became central players at the court. Late in the year, after a few turbulent months, they succeeded in closing off an exclusive circle around the King whose third man was Peter Schumacher—later Griffenfeld—a commoner who had enjoyed a cometlike career at the court of Frederik III; Schumacher had been Frederik's librarian and had written the Royal Law of 1665. This trio monopolised power during the years that followed; the King made decisions after having consulted Gyldenløve and Ahlefeldt, while it was Schumacher who more or less kept the machinery of state running.

The system of ranks and the new nobility

Schumacher was also the main architect behind three laws that established the social ground rules that would be applicable during the reign of Christian V. The laws radically redefined the hierarchy under the King.

First came the so-called Chamber Ordinance of 11 May 1670, which, on a purely practical level, regulated the access to His Majesty that was sought by so many. If one could secure an audience, the King might prove to be gracious and grant one or the other of one's requests, but otherwise one had to go through middlemen such as Gyldenløve or Schumacher, and they expected to be, and were, paid well. The Chamber Ordinance defined who could enter the first and second antechamber, and

functions both at the royal court and in Norway, where he represented the King from 1664 until 1699. He was the son of Margrethe Pape, with whom Frederik III had had a relationship in his youth.

In the course of a few decades, Christian V's system of rankings became so complicated that almost no one could maintain an overview over it any longer, but these crowns illustrate the uppermost ranks in the late seventeenth century. At the top, of course, we have the King and the Queen; then come the Crown Prince and Crown Princess and the other princes and princesses, followed by the Golden Lions (the kings' "natural" children), the counts, and the "free gentlemen" (the barons), after whom come the old nobility, who are, then, theoretically beneath the new nobility.

Shirt of red silk velvet, the pattern on which is sewn with silver thread and includes the Order of the Dannebrog, the Order of the Elephant, and Christian V's monogram. This shirt presents the King in his role as a reformer of the system of knightly orders.

now the nobility could not proceed further than to the second antechamber.

The two other laws were published on 25 May 1671 and meant that at the same time the Chamber Ordinance had to be revised. Now, with the advent of the Counts' and Barons' Privileges, an entirely new class of nobility was created: this legislation determined who could be admitted to the so-called titled nobility, as opposed to the old birth nobility. With the new titles Count and Baron came privileges that were reminiscent of the privileges the old nobility had had prior to the introduction of absolute monarchy. The law, then, was a further assault on the traditional privileges of the nobility.

In addition, there was the so-called Rank Ordinance, a long list of names and titles that established who had a right to walk, stand, and sit in front of whom on public occasions. At the top of this list were the King's "natural sons" (that is, Gyldenløverne, "the Golden Lions"), at the bottom the chancellery secretaries. The key to securing a place in the rankings was public office, and this was the case regardless of whether one was a nobleman or not. Of course it was possible for members of the nobility to acquire honorary titles—normally in return for payment—and thus acquire a place in the rankings, but the decree threatened individuals who failed to observe the new rankings with stiff fines, and this threat was clearly addressed to the nobility in particular.

The three laws bear witness to the fact that the old nobility were suspected of wanting to overthrow the absolute monarchy during the years that immediately preceded and immediately followed Christian V's accession to the throne and that Christian V and

Chain of the Order of the Dannebrog with order badge of gold with enamel and table-cut stones. The Order of the Dannebrog was established on 12 October 1671, the day after the birth of Crown Prince Frederik (IV), and was motivated by the desire to have a modern knightly order that could be given to anyone the King found deserving. Christian V claimed that he was renewing an order established by Valdemar Sejr in the thirteenth century, which was complete fiction.

his inner circle wanted to neutralise this threat by redefining what it was that conferred status in the society. Being from a fine family became of secondary importance in a system in which the most important parameters were whether one had an official position within the apparatus of the state and whether one enjoyed the favour of the King. By implementing the new rankings system, the absolute monarchy got people to use their energy to get into the system or to climb in the rankings. Loyalty thus became a decisive factor in connection with the acquisition of social status, and the new laws in fact made it possible to establish a loyal elite around the King that was practically free of connections to the old nobility as a locus of power.

The anointment

It was not a coincidence that the new laws were proclaimed a few weeks before Christian V's anointment ceremony on 7 June 1671. The new hierarchy was confirmed at this ceremony, which formally demonstrated who was at its top. The inspiration came from the anointments of kings described in the Old Testament, and the custom had been observed since the Middle Ages, but while until now the anointment (application of a salve on the wrist, chest, and forehead as a symbol of the power of God) had been a component of the coronation ceremony, it became the central act in the context of the absolute monarchy. Indeed, the ceremony was moved from the Church of Our Lady to Frederiksborg Palace Church, and only individuals who had been specially invited were present. The reason given for this was that the anointment was a "devotional act" in which the King simply confirmed his piety and God-fearing nature, but of course it was the King's intention that the event would attract the attention of the people and that people should read the descriptions that were subsequently published.

Before and after it took place, the anointment was referred to as a "coronation," but this was precisely what it was not, for the most important symbolic innovation was that the King placed the crown on his head himself. Previously, the members of the Council of the Realm had set the crown on the King's head and thus demonstrated that it was they who granted the King his authority. There had been a similar symbolic content in the fact that the members of the Council of the Realm had carried the regalia (the sceptre, the orb, etc.) to the ceremony and only transferred them to the King after the ceremony had been completed, but now the King brought the regalia to the ceremony himself. This, too, underscored that the anointment actu-

Christian V's anointment in Frederiksborg Palace Church in 1671, depicted by Michael van Haven. The picture is a sketch for a copper plate etching, and the size of the church's interior, which is actually a fairly cramped space, has been greatly exaggerated.

Coronation cape of red silk velvet, embroidered in gold thread with 1,400 royal crowns and edged with ermine, though the lining is white rabbit fur. Christian V wore this cape at his anointment ceremony in 1671, and it was used for the same purpose by all the kings of the absolute monarchy.

ally did not play any role whatsoever in establishing Christian V's qualifications to be King; rather, the anointment simply emphasised his power within a religious context.

There was, however, a problem with regard to the treatment of the Queen. Because of her Reformed faith, Charlotte Amalie refused to go to the altar and receive the sacrament together with her husband prior to the anointment, and for this reason, it was not considered appropriate for her to be anointed. Peter Schumacher

Christian V's crown was made by Paul Kurtz in Copenhagen in 1670 and 1671, and the King wore it for the first time at his anointment. All the kings of the absolute monarchy used it in connection with their anointments, and it was last worn by Christian VIII in 1840. Since the adoption of the constitution of 1849, the monarch has been neither crowned nor anointed, but the crown is still used in connection with the death of the monarch: it is placed on the coffin as a component of the castrum doloris. The crown weighs two kilograms, and the precious stones were probably taken from older jewellery. The sapphire on the front of the crown, for example, can be traced back to Frederik I.

came up with the idea of justifying the Queen's lack of anointment by proclaiming that because of her marriage to the hereditary King, she was already "completely crowned," and he thus elegantly transformed an embarrassing problem into an expression of the self-understanding of the hereditary absolute monarchy.

The actual ceremony lasted a good four hours, much of which time was spent emphasising the monarchy's divine character and the King's religious duties. The Royal Law was once again read aloud, and afterward, there was a formal dinner at which the King was served in a separate room together with the Queen and the King's brother, Prince Jørgen, while the highest-ranking courtiers participated in serving the royal family.

Could probably be fit together Amethyst in setting with Christian V's double initial in gold on enamel, possibly executed by Paul Kurtz in 1671. The jewel had been worn by Frederik III on the occasion of his coronation in 1648, and it was subsequently worn when the King sat on the throne during the anointment.

Bowl of semiprecious heliotrope that belonged to Queen Charlotte Amalie and is engraved with her monogram. The four lions can be interpreted as a reference to the lion on the coat of arms of Hesse, which has here been coated with the blue colour of the Order of the Elephant. The Queen collected handicrafts in materials including rock crystal and semiprecious stones, and she herself was competent in several handicrafts, including embroidery and the turning of ivory.

The queen and the mistress

One of the customs that must have made an impression on the young Crown Prince when he visited the court of Louis XIV was the French king's well-known relationship with a maitresse, that is, a mistress. Shortly following his accession to the throne, in any event, he began a relationship with the sixteen-year-old Sophie Amalie Moth, whose father was the King's former teacher Poul Moth, who had been Frederik III's personal physician. She only gradually acquired the status of an official mistress, but in 1671—the year Crown Prince Frederik (IV) was born—the King bought a house right next to the palace for Sophie Amalie Moth. The following year,

she gave birth to Christian V's first extramarital child, and a further five children followed in the course of the next ten years. In 1676, Christian V gave her the island of Samsø, and the following year, he made her the Countess of Samsø, which elevated her not only to the nobility but indeed to its very top. In 1679, the King publicly declared that he was the father of the children, and they subsequently bore the title Gyldenløve ("Golden Lion").

It was nothing new for a king to have extramarital affairs or recognise the children that resulted from such affairs, but it was new that the King made his mistress a noblewoman. It was also without precedent that the King had a mistress while he was officially married to Charlotte Amalie and that the Queen and the King's mistress had children who were about the same age.

The Queen certainly must have found this state of affairs humiliating, perhaps in particular because of the difficulties she had experienced during her first years in Denmark. There had been no pregnancies, which had put the Queen under significant pressure, and at the same time, Charlotte Amalie had had to confront religious hostility and a stepmother with a hostile attitude. In Christian V's defence, however, it could be noted that royal marriages were arranged without any expectation that emotional attachments between the parties would develop, and in fact, the royal couple's relationship nevertheless appears to have functioned well alongside the King's family life with Sophie Amalie Moth. The royal couple enjoyed playing cards together for hours, and during the period 1671–87, the Queen gave birth to eight children, which does suggest that the royal couple got along well together, the obvious element of duty notwithstanding. Also, the Queen's position at court was never threatened by Sophie Amalie Moth, who kept her distance even when she discreetly followed the royal couple on their travels around the country.

In keeping with tradition, Christian V took care of his "natural" sons. Christian Gyldenløve, who was born in 1674, was appointed the head of Bergen Parish when he was three years old and made the head of the Norwegian postal service when he was six; when Christian Gyldenløve was eleven, the latter post was passed on to his younger brother Ulrik Christian Gyldenløve, who had been born in 1678, and Christian Gyldenløve himself became the head of the Danish postal service. Of course, these posts did not imply a responsibility to work; they simply provided income. These two sons were also given officers' commissions at high ranks when they were still quite young, and in 1685, they were officially received at the palace to-

Flower picture by the German painter, botanist, and entomologist Maria Sibylla Merian (1647–1717), whose studies of insects and flowers were far ahead of their time. During the reign of Christian V, Rosenborg acquired a fine collection consisting of fifty drawings, probably illustrations from her first great work on flowers.

gether with their sister Christiane. Until that point, Charlotte Amalie had refused to see the children of "die Moth," as she called her, and she demanded and got substantial compensation for receiving them. In part, this compensation took the form of approval of the construction of the Reformed Church Charlotte Amalie had long wished to have built; the church was built right across from Rosenborg, where it still stands today. In addition, Charlotte Amalie was able to secure freedom of religion for members of the Reformed Church, who were emigrating from France in large numbers during this period because of their persecution by Louis XIV, and many of whom settled in Denmark.

The two women in the King's life shared the fate of having to bury most of their children. At that time, many short lives were lived. Two of Sophie Amalie Moth's daughters died of dysentery in 1684, and two others died during a smallpox epidemic in 1689. In fact, Ulrik Christian Gyldenløve was the only one of her children who survived the King's mistress, and he died in 1719, the year of her death. Of the eight children who resulted from Christian V's marriage to Charlotte Amalie, it was only Crown Prince Frederik (1672–1730), Princess Sophie Hedevig (1677–1735) and Prince Carl (1680–1729) who did not die very young. A son and a daughter died in infancy, a daughter died at ten during the abovementioned smallpox epidemic and two sons—Prince Vilhelm and Prince Carl—lived to be eighteen and twenty years old, respectively.

The rise and fall of Griffenfeld

Getting absolute monarchy to work in practice was not quite as easy as it might sound. The King was in charge, but if he would have handled every matter himself, he would have lost his overview and drowned in tasks. If he delegated too much to advisors and officials, however, it would be possible to question whether or not he in fact held absolute power. The challenge was to find a form of government that on the one hand secured the King's right to control the state's affairs and on the other hand kept the burden of work from increasing to an unacceptable level. All absolute monarchs faced this dilemma, and Christian V never found a viable solution.

During the first years of his reign, however, he tested a solution that consisted of allowing a single particularly trusted individual to take on most of the work. Such an individual was known as a favourite, and there were a number of them at the royal

Peter Schumacher, the Count of Griffenfeld (1635–99), painted on wood by Abraham Wuchters around 1671.

Christian V aims at the head of a "Moor" (an African) during a carousel ride. Carousel riding was a less risky replacement for the knightly tournaments of the Middle Ages; the point was to hit various objects with various weapons during a series of "games." These were splendid shows in which the King and the other riders—the realm's absolute elite—demonstrated their superiority with magnificent costumes and splendid horses. To avoid any doubt, it should be noted that this was not the head of a real human being but of a dummy.

courts of the seventeenth century, the French cardinals Richelieu and Mazarin being especially famous examples. Christian V found his favourite in Peter Schumacher, who reached a position of such power that he practically became Denmark's actual ruler himself.

Schumacher was the son of a wine merchant, but in the new system he himself had participated in creating, this was not of primary importance. For Christian V, it was more important that Schumacher was a master of rhetoric with an enormous capacity for work and a corresponding ability to maintain an overview, and his influence increased rapidly. During the year 1670, Schumacher got the procedures of the central administration changed so that all matters had to pass by him before they reached the King, and he also became the secretary of the newly created Privy Council. In connection with the anointment of the King, Schumacher received a diamond-studded portrait of the King; in July 1671, he was made a member of the new nobility under the name Griffenfeld. In September, he became a member of the Privy Council with full rights, and in October, he was among the first recipients of the new Order of the Dannebrog.

His rise had been made possible by the previously mentioned alliance with Ahlefeldt and particularly Gyldenløve, but he ultimately outshone both of them. In 1673, Griffenfeld was made a count, and the following year, he became the head of both chancelleries with the title of Chancellor of the Realm as well as President of the Supreme Court. One could say he became an all-dominating prime minister. Griffenfeld not only determined which matters would be brought to the King but also what decisions would be made with regard to these matters; to the greatest extent possible, he remained in the immediate vicinity of the King. In addition, Griffenfeld was a master of extravagant elegance, and his home in Købmagergade displayed a carefully staged magnificence that was exceeded only by the homes of the members of the royal family.

In his supreme confidence in his own power, however, Griffenfeld gradually forgot that even his own position was dependent on the favour of the King. He certainly acted on the basis of his own highly personal sense of what was in Christian V's interests when, during the years leading up to the Scanian War, he attempted to insist on peaceable policy that conflicted with the King's wish to win back what his father had lost. Griffenfeld maintained a diplomatic course in relation to France, which was allied with Sweden, and while Christian V was a great admirer of Louis XIV, a revenge war was his top priority.

For Christian V, it was probably the last straw that some of Griffenfeld's enemies, of which Griffenfeld had gradually acquired many, got hold of a letter that indicated that even after the outbreak of war, Griffenfeld had kept open a line of communication with France. The King had already been in the process of losing his trust in Griffenfeld; in a famous letter written the previous year, Christian V had made it clear that he felt he was being manipulated. This letter had been a friendly warning; while the King certainly liked the Chancellor of the Realm, he perceived Griffenfeld's

Christian V's breastplate and helmet. The set is made of gilded brass and was used for carousel riding. Note the elephants on the shoulders and helmet, which are references to the royal order.

headstrong course as an attempt to seize actual governmental power. There were others who saw things this way as well, which gave the King a strong reason to set an example. The war itself was another reason; in the tense situation the war created, it was much easier to perceive Griffenfeld's behaviour as traitorous—particularly because he had the military leadership against him.

On 11 March 1676, Griffenfeld was arrested on his way to the palace, and during the following months he was subjected to a real show trial that ended with his being sentenced to loss of life, honour and property for treason, acceptance of bribes and the selling of official positions. The sentence might well have been reduced if Griffenfeld had admitted his full or partial guilt, but he denied the truth of any of the charges. While the charge of treason was not justifiable, it was true that Griffenfeld had exploited his position for personal gain. Bribery was common, but the Chancellor of the Realm had systematised corruption and had been careless with regard to destroying evidence. It was very practical that the fortune Griffenfeld had amassed in this manner could be used to cover the deficit in the budget for Denmark's navy.

The execution of Griffenfeld was stayed at the last moment, when he literally lay with his head on the block, but the fallen favourite had to spend the rest of his life in prison—the first fourteen years at the Citadel and the years from 1680 until 1698 in the fortress of Munkholm near Trondheim. He was given no writing utensils, for it would of course not have been in Christian V's interests for such a gifted rhetorician to have written his memoirs in his captivity.

After having toppled Griffenfeld, Christian V declared that he would thenceforth be his own prime minister—this was the same declaration Louis XIV had made upon the death of Cardinal Mazarin in 1661. The day after the arrest, he called the foreign envoys to the palace and instructed them to address their enquiries directly to him in the future; the Danish envoys abroad were given the same instruction. In addition, Christian V took it upon himself to open all letters that had been received himself from now on, so for the most part, he took on the overall responsibility for foreign policy. This gave him a significantly greater amount of work, and not surprisingly, it turned out that in general Christian V was not able to rule with nearly the same firmness as Griffenfeld. The leadership of the state was to a greater extent characterised by uncertainty, the formation of blocs and intrigues, and things continued more or less like this for the rest of the King's life.

Next spread: Tapestry in the Great Hall at Rosenborg Palace. Christian V had the twelve so-called Rosenborg tapestries woven during the period 1685–93; the tapestries show the Danish-Norwegian victories during the Scanian War. Ironically enough, the Swedish king ordered a corresponding set of tapestries depicting the Swedish victories. This tapestry shows Christian V receiving the surrender of the city of Wismar on 13 December 1675, after the city had endured a siege lasting a month and a half. On the right, at the bottom of the hill, Queen Charlotte Amalie can be seen in a carriage.

The Scanian War

One effect of the fall of Griffenfeld was certainly that it became possible to implement consistent policy with regard to the war that was already in progress. For Christian V, the revenge war must have appeared to be the challenge of his life, and there were several reasons why it had now become a reality.

At the time of Christian V's accession to the throne, Sweden was in a strong position and had no interest in a new war. The Swedes even had a foothold inside the borders of the realm, as the House of Gottorp was very friendly towards Sweden. The House of Gottorp was a side branch of the Danish royal family that had authority over scattered areas within the duchies of Schleswig and Holstein. The Duke of Gottorp had been given full sovereignty by the Treaty of Roskilde thanks to Swedish pressure, so the Danish king, one could say, had a hostile state within his own borders. For Christian V, it was a given that this threat had to be eliminated, so he tried to force Gottorp in Schleswig to accept a takeover, but all he achieved in this way was to get the Duke of Gottorp to conclude a formal defensive alliance with Sweden.

There were much greater powers involved, however, for the power relationships in the Baltic region had gradually become an integrated part of the politics of great European kingdoms. When Louis XIV initiated a war against the Netherlands in 1672, it was almost unavoidable that this war would involve the Nordic powers. This had to do with the fact that small states such as Denmark-Norway were interested in forming alliances that required them to go to war in return for receiving subsidies (that is, financial support) from the great powers. The subsidies gave military strategies a special character, as they caused small states' internal wars to be influenced by the systems of alliances with which they were associated. During the years that followed the French declaration of war, two alliances were formed, one of which included France, Sweden, and Hanover, the other the Netherlands, Brandenburg, the Emperor (Austria), Spain, and Brunswick-Lüneburg. Denmark joined the latter alliance in 1674, and the war in the Baltic region began the same year when Sweden attacked Brandenburg. Christian V declared war on Sweden the same year, after the Netherlands had done so.

Denmark made its first move in the summer of 1675, occupying Gottorp. Around the same time, the fighting for Bohuslän in Norway began, and Denmark subsequently participated in an attack on the Swedish part of Pomerania. When the sailing season

began in March 1676, the sea war began as well. In the summer, new fronts were opened up. Troops from Denmark and Lüneburg marched into Swedish-controlled Bremen-Verden, an area in Northern Germany Frederik III had lost when he had been a prince-bishop. Fighting in central Norway also began, as did the war in Scania, which for Denmark became the primary battleground of the war.

The crossing to Scania required naval support, and it proved to be possible to bring an army of fourteen thousand men safely across the Øresund after a Danish-Dutch fleet had defeated the Swedish fleet at the battle of Øland on 1 July 1676. After some initial Danish successes, the Danish and Swedish main forces collided at Lund on 4 December 1676. This battle was one of the bloodiest ever fought in the Nordic region; the Danes suffered the most casualties, losing eight thousand soldiers, while the Swedes lost six thousand. After this battle, it turned out to be practically impossible to conquer and defend Scania, but the war continued, and thousands of soldiers were slaughtered in a series of more minor battles—for example, Christian V lost four thousand men when he attempted to take Malmö following a siege in June 1677. The fortunes of war shifted back and forth, and Scanian guerrilla warriors—the so-called snapphanes—created an extra challenge to the Swedes, but the Swedes nevertheless ended up controlling almost all of Scania when the war

Cup of rock crystal, cut in the shape of a flying fish. Presented to Christian V by his mother Sophie Amalie on the occasion of the conquest of Wismar. Executed in Milan around 1580.

was over. The Scanians were the biggest losers, for the forces on both sides acted ruthlessly and without consideration for the best interests of the populace. The Danish troops did not hesitate to adopt a scorched earth policy during their retreat, and eventually the enthusiasm with which they had been received by their former countrymen was significantly reduced.

The sea war was almost entirely separate from the land war, and the Danes were much more successful at sea than on land. At the Battle of Møn on 1 June 1677, the Danish fleet captured several Swedish ships, and a month later, on 1 July, the Danes won control of the seas in the Battle of Køge Bay. A Swedish fleet of twenty-five ships of the line and eleven frigates was met by a Danish fleet of nineteen ships of the line and six frigates under the command of Niels Juel. By means of an extremely daring manoeuvre, he was able to put the numerically inferior Danish fleet in a tactically advantageous position so that he could capture seven Swedish ships of the line and sink several others. This victory meant that the Swedish fleet would be unable to fight effectively for the remainder of the war—and that Niels Juel would achieve immortality as a naval hero.

However, the final result of the war was not determined in battle at all; rather, it was dictated by France. Louis XIV had not succeeded in conquering the Netherlands, and in the summer of 1678, a peace treaty was negotiated between France on the one hand and the Netherlands and Spain on the other. Early in 1679 a peace treaty between Austria and Lüneburg was also concluded, and in the summer of that year, Brandenburg concluded a peace treaty with France and Sweden, the conditions of which were imposed by France. After this, Denmark and Sweden were the only warring parties, and Christian V ended up having to accept a peace treaty after France had occupied Oldenburg and was threatening to invade the duchies. The peace treaty dictated that Denmark-Norway would have to give up all the conquered areas: Gottorp, Gotland, Rügen, Wismar, Bremen, and Verden as well as parts of Bohuslän in Norway. Neither France nor the Netherlands desired a weakened Sweden, so they enforced a return to the conditions established by the Treaty of Roskilde of 1658. Ultimately all Christian V achieved with this war was the demonstration of his ability to match Denmark's archrival in a military context.

This demonstration had been seen not least in Norway, where an almost independent part of the war had taken place. Ulrik Frederik Gyldenløve had been in Norway since he had been outmanoeuvred at court in 1673, and because of his involvement,

Portrait of Christian V's sister, Queen Ulrika Eleonora of Sweden, painted by D. Klöcker Ehrenstrahl. With support from Griffenfeld and Dowager Queen Sophie Amalie, Ulrika Eleonora became engaged to the young Swedish king Charles XI in the summer of 1675. A marriage did not become a reality before war was declared, but both Ulrika Eleonora herself and the Swedish king rejected alternative suggestions, and the marriage contract was signed together with the peace treaty at Lund. The alliance never had any political significance, but it testifies to the fact that there were strong supporters of a policy of Danish-Swedish alliance in both countries.

this part of the war is referred to as the Gyldenløve Feud in Norwegian tradition. In Norway, there were disputes over borders but also actual campaigns in Bohuslän, where the Norwegian forces were competently led by the King's half-brother.

Christian V himself also won a good deal of honour in the war. He fought well in the Battle of Lund and the Battle of Landskrona, and in fact he would be the last Danish king who personally went into battle. This is not to say that the King fought on the front line like a common soldier, but he took on the role of commander-in-chief in the field. Of course, it was not entirely sensible for a king to risk life and limb in this way, but it did serve further to increase the King's great popularity among his subjects.

The postwar period

Despite the fact that both Denmark-Norway and Sweden presented the results of the war as a victory, both parties were in a way the losers of the war. Arguably, the war's real victors were the great powers that dictated the terms of the peace, for by weakening each other the two Nordic realms had only opened the Baltic region to more influence from without. The Scanian War contributed to integrating the Nordic region into a greater European political system.

The remainder of the century was characterised by continuing conflicts in which Louis XIV, who wished to incorporate into France contested areas on his borders, had almost all the rest of Europe against him. Sweden had had enough of French authoritarianism and allied itself with France's enemies. Denmark-Norway had to find a place within this pattern, and Christian V would not have an easy time of it.

During the first postwar years, Denmark attached itself to France, as having a good relationship with France would be of decisive importance if Denmark was to succeed in absorbing Gottorp into the realm. France had implied that it would not hinder this, so in 1684, Christian V, inspired by Louis XIV's aggressive border policies, incorporated Gottorp's territories in Schleswig into Schleswig itself so that these territories came to be under the King's control. Five years later, however, the King was forced to restore the Duke of Gottorp's old rights. This was partly because Christian V had somewhat recklessly attacked Hamburg and thus provoked the anger of the Northern German princes but also partly because Denmark in fact ended up receiving no support from France when such support was needed. Because of this, Denmark's relationship with France cooled off again while Sweden's influence in Gottorp became even stronger, setting the stage for Christian V's son Frederik IV and the Great Northern War.

The Danish Code, the Norwegian Code, and the Great Land Survey

The 1670s were certainly the most dramatic decade during Christian V's reign, but the 1680s were the decade during which the most lasting changes took place. The constantly growing government of the realm demanded better administration and not least dependable revenues. The strengthening of central power during this period was achieved by means of a number of measures, of which only the most impor-

Next spread:
Ole Rømer's Room at Rosenborg. The astronomer Ole Rømer (1644–1710), who calculated the speed of light, became an important figure at the court of Christian V after he returned to Denmark from Paris, where he had lived for many years, in 1681. Rømer's contributions included the standardization of weights and measures, and in the background, one can see a row of weights of bronze, the so-called "national prototypes" that established the new weight standards. In the foreground a machine can be seen that displays the orbits of the planets (a planetarium) and another machine, one for calculating lunar eclipses (an "eclipsarium"), which Rømer invented and presented to the Royal Danish Academy of Sciences and Letters in Paris in 1680.

tant will be mentioned here: the codification of existing law and the restructuring of the tax system.

Immediately after the introduction of absolute monarchy, Frederik III had established a committee that was to eliminate the laws that were not compatible with absolute monarchy, and it had proved to be necessary to develop new comprehensive complexes of laws that could replace the old regional legislation (the Law of Jutland, the Law of Zealand, and the Law of Scania) as well as the recesses (sets of laws with mixed contents) of previous centuries. The project was delayed by years of interruptions, but Christian V could finally present the Danish Code in 1683 and the very similarly worded Norwegian Code in 1687. On the one hand, the Laws were a work of compilation that included revised elements of the old Laws and of the håndfæstninger of the electoral monarchy to the extent such elements were compatible with the absolute monarchy. On the other hand, the Danish Code and the Norwegian Code, which featured a great deal of new content and a high degree of uniformity, represented a clear break with the messy myriad of laws that had traditionally existed in Denmark. The new laws provided a comprehensible legal basis for the exercise of power by the centralised absolute monarchy and for the most part remained in effect for the remainder of the age of absolute monarchy.

The new basis for the collection of taxes was no less important. Traditionally, the revenues of the state had come from the crown's land and from customs payments, but a large part of the crown's land had been sold during the reign of Frederik III, and the Øresund tariffs were providing less money than they had earlier—not least because the Treaty of Roskilde had granted Swedish ships exemption from paying duties. For this reason, there was only one way to go if the state was to be adequately financed, and that was to raise taxes. The need to increase taxes was by no means lessened by the fact that a large and costly professional army was being maintained in Denmark in the wake of the Scanian War, while in Norway the army was still based on conscripted soldiers. The rural population had to make a substantial contribution to footing the bill, so while an average farm had paid three to four rigsdaler per year in taxes around 1660, the same farm was paying closer to twenty rigsdaler when Christian V died. The dramatically increased level of taxation created a need for an optimised basis, so during the 1680s, all agricultural land in Denmark (except on Bornholm) was measured and evaluated. The result was Christian V's Danish Land Survey of 1688—an impressive piece of work that for us today constitutes the most important contemporary source of information about agriculture in Denmark during the period.

A prerequisite for the dramatic increase in taxes was that under the absolute monarchy commoners had been granted the right to purchase land. The landowning class therefore included an increasing number of commoners and members of the new nobility, who in fact came to possess more land than the old nobility during Christian V's reign. The new landowners were loyal to the King, which made it easier for Christian V to leave both the administration of taxation and—in Norway—the administration of military conscription to the landowners. The landowners were made responsible for ensuring that the full amount was paid and the required number of soldiers were provided. For this reason, it was in the landowners' own interests to

The Danish coat of arms with order chains and wild men, executed in enamelled silver in 1693.

Portrait of Christian
V by Jacob d'Agar
from around 1690.

Portrait of Queen Charlotte Amalie by Jacob d'Agar from around 1690. The little person on the Queen's left side is the Queen's court dwarf Elsgen. At the time, it was a common custom at the royal courts of Europe to keep dwarves, who, like black servants and unusual animals such as monkeys and parrots, contributed to making life at court seem exotic and magical. However, Elsgen was not simply an amusing item of inventory. She was one of the Queen's closest confidantes and had her own armchair in the Queen's chamber.

Two flintlock rifles signed "Lars Berrig Trundheim." Pictures and inscriptions related to Christian V's journey to Norway in 1685 have been added to the stocks. The King impressed many people he encountered on this journey, for example, by fearlessly carrying out mine inspections and by making his way up steep mountainsides on horseback. The rifles are richly inlaid with costly materials. The spring-loaded flintlock, which was simple to use and very dependable, was a new invention that quickly became the dominant rifle type.

take care of the state's business, and in this way, the state acquired an inexpensive administration that could effectively collect the high taxes imposed on the farmers.

A famous contemporary source of information on Christian V's last years is An Account of Denmark as It Was in the Year 1692 by Robert Molesworth, an English diplomat. This work is based on his own experiences at the Danish court. As an English liberal, Molesworth was strongly critical of absolute monarchy. In his view, the Danish system was a despotic one in which the King's subjects were forced to pay taxes that financed military forces that not only functioned as a war machine but also as an instrument of oppression within Denmark. However, Molesworth had to admit that the laws of the realm as formulated in the Danish/Norwegian Code were exemplary in their clarity and concision, and he found that the basic structure of the absolute state was solid.

The dream of a palace

Power had thus been consolidated, but there was not as much splendour as Christian V would have liked. It is almost impossible to overstate the importance of staging for the early absolute monarchy, as splendour was the visible expression of the King's power and was interpreted as such both by foreign envoys and by the Danish upper class. For the common populace, the royals must have appeared to be like beings from another planet, but there was no reason not to maintain this impression.

Christian V presiding at the Supreme Court, where, as the absolute monarch, he was the highest judge. The Supreme Court was established by Frederik III in 1661 and met once a year, eight days after Pentecost. Here, in theory, any of the King's subjects could present their cases before the King, though of course in reality there was a selection process. The painting is probably from 1697 and hangs in its original place in Rosenborg Palace.

Hunt scene executed in papier mâché by Christian van Bracht, who was an employee of the hunt-loving King. The theme of a court masquerade in 1693 was that the costumes should reflect favourite pastimes, and Christian V's costume made reference to hunting, lovemaking, and war.

France had set a standard all European royal courts tried to live up to, and the French language was used at these courts—including at the Danish court, though here German remained the primary language. Christian V did not have enough money to match the French example, so he had to prioritise. He kept day-to-day costs, particularly his personal expenses, low to the greatest extent possible but spent a great deal of money on representation. Receptions for ambassadors, for example, were thoroughly choreographed displays in which every effort was made to impress the respective guest.

However, there was no getting around having the King's fine guests report to their home countries that the royal residence, Copenhagen Castle, did not meet the standards of the age by any stretch of the imagination. The medieval castle with its various additions seemed cramped and old-fashioned, and the absolute monarchy need-

The rack of antlers from the stag that injured Christian V so severely in 1698 that the King died the following year.

ed a splendid palace. Christian V had several plans prepared for a new residence on the property where his mother's pleasure palace Sophie Amalienborg had stood until it had burned down in 1689. The site was obviously appropriate for an ambitious construction project, but such a project did not become a reality until the 1750s, when the current Amalienborg Palace was built.

The organ with the splendid limewood facade in the Church of Our Saviour in Copenhagen is one of the best-known Danish musical instruments. During the reigns of both Christian IV and Frederik III, there were plans for the construction of a church in Christianshavn—a part of the city that was founded by Christian IV—but such plans were not to be realized until the time of Christian V, who had the Church of Our Saviour built in the 1690s. The distinctive twisting spire was added to the building during the reign of Frederik V. Christian V also financed the organ, the mild and fatherly centrepiece of which is the bust of the King. The organ is dated 1698, and some of the original organ pipes are still playing!

In a secret testament addressed to Crown Prince Frederik (IV), Christian V expressed his regret that because of war and other disadvantageous circumstances he had not built a palace that would glorify the monarchy. For similar reasons, however, his son, too, would pass the task on, so it would be Christian VI who finally made the splendid palace of the absolute monarchy a reality in the form of the first Christiansborg Palace.

Throughout his life, Christian V had been plagued by coughing, and in his last years his health was poor, but this did not prevent him from going hunting. However, the

King's beloved hobby ended up costing him his life. One autumn day in 1698, while he was eating his lunch at the Hubertus House, the predecessor of the Hermitage Palace, the King was informed that an exhausted red deer was nearby. The King was seriously injured in connection with giving the deer the coup de grâce, and after having suffered from the effects of this injury for the better part of a year, he died at Copenhagen Castle on 25 August 1699.

The legacy

Christian V has never attracted great interest from historians. And indeed there is no doubt that as a ruler he was less remarkable than, for example, his predecessor and his successor. Unlike Louis XIV, he did not become an incarnation of the absolutist state that formed around him, but Christian V contributed to giving his state a durable basic structure, and the extant daily records and writings he produced bear witness to his energetic involvement in all matters of state. He consolidated the ab-

Gyldenløve's Palace seen from the garden side in 1694. The view is toward Kongens Nytorv, and the ship on the right is in Nyhavn, "the New Harbour." Today the grey building behind the ship is the French embassy. After Christian V's death, Charlotte Amalie bought the palace, the construction of which Ulrik Frederik Gyldenløve had launched in 1672—at the time when he, Frederik Ahlefeldt, and Peter Schumacher had been a powerful trio constituting the inner circle around Christian V. The palace became the residence of the Dowager Queen until her death in 1814, and it was named Charlottenborg after her.

Detail of a view of Copenhagen from the northwest, toward Nørreport. Watercolour drawing from the late seventeenth century, signed Wickenn Riboldt. Within the

solutist state and thus succeeded in completing what was arguably the most important task he had inherited.

In Danish historiography, there has been a tradition of portraying Christian V as a little dumber than he probably was. This is likely due in particular to the King's lack of interest in book-learning, something that is of course greatly valued by historians themselves, but it could also be partly because he has been compared with the extremely gifted Peter Griffenfeld. Despite his fall from power, Griffenfeld has gone down in Danish history as an honoured individual, for as long as the absolute monarchy lasted Griffenfeld could

be hailed as the author of the Royal Law and as a commoner who transcended the usual patterns in great style. Crown Prince Frederik (IV) was already a declared admirer of Griffenfeld and would have released him if the prisoner had not died shortly before Frederik acceded to the throne in 1699. A tradition developed of viewing the Chancellor of the Realm as a misunderstood genius whose unusual abilities provoked the envy of less talented individuals and whom the King let himself be manipulated into toppling because the King did not see that pursuing peace would have been the best path for Denmark to take. It appears just as justifiable to conclude that Griffenfeld misread the situation and overplayed his hand, but the result of the war showed that he had been right.

fortifications, farthest to the left, Rosenborg can be seen. The little tower closest to Rosenborg is the Reformed Church— Charlotte Amalie's special contribution to the capital city.

The pitiful remains of a wax bust of Christian V. A handsomely worked torso made for the Art Chamber in the 1680s. Like several of Christian V's outfits, the bust, which features a hump behind the right shoulder blade, suggests that the King was humpbacked. In his last years, he sometimes used a wheelchair, which might have been because of pain associated with this condition.

After all, Christian V's military project was not successful, and while in the 1680s the King pursued the same goals as in the Scanian War by other means, the great prize remained out of reach. Despite the historically far-reaching reforms he implemented in the course of his reign, the unsuccessful war ended up preventing the King's reign from appearing in an entirely positive light, and the King is likely to have seen things this way himself. For regardless of how much the kings of the past might have been praised for their mildness and piety, and regardless of how good a man Christian V might have been, military triumphs remained the top priority for an absolute monarch.

SUGGESTIONS FOR FURTHER READING

Knud Fabricius (ed.), *Danmarks Konger*, Jespersen og Pios Forlag 1944. There are not many dedicated biographical presentations of Christian V, but there is an excellent one in this work from the time of the German occupation of Denmark. The book has a modern and highly recommendable successor in Knud J.V. Jespersen et al., *Danmarks konger og dronninger*, Gyldendal Leksikon 2004.

Thomas Lyngby, Søren Mentz, and Sebastian Olden-Jørgensen, *Magt og Pragt – Enevælde 1660–1848,* Gads Forlag 2010.
A kind of basic textbook on the Danish absolute monarchy that also offers a broad view of the rest of Europe during the period in question.

Sebastian Olden-Jørgensen, *Kun navnet er tilbage – En biografi om Peter Griffenfeld,* Gads Forlag 1999.
A scholarly and also very entertaining book about Griffenfeld's unusual fate.

Ståle Dyrvik, *Truede tvillingriker 1648–1720,* Volume III of the series *Danmark-Norge* 1380–1814, Universitetsforlaget 1998.
An excellent scholarly overview in Norwegian that, naturally enough, emphasizes a Norwegian perspective more than many Danish historiographic works.

Katia Johansen and Peter Kristiansen, *Rosenborgtapeterne / The Rosenborg Tapestries,* De danske kongers kronologiske samling 1999.
A little book on the tapestries owned by Christian V that depict his victories in the Scanian War. Published on the occasion of the return of the tapestries to the Great Hall at Rosenborg after they had hung at Christiansborg for many years.

www.kongernessamling.dk.

Christian V
The first heir to the throne

Copyright © 2017
The Royal Danish Collection and Historika / Gads Forlag A/S

ISBN: 978-87-93229-71-6
First edition, first print run

Printed in Lithuania

Text: Jens Gunni Busck
Edited by Birgit Jenvold
Translated from Danish by Peter Sean Woltemade
Cover and graphic design Lene Nørgaard, Le Bureau
Printed by Clemenstrykkeriet, Lithuania

Illustrations:
Front page, p. 2 (photo: Iben Kaufmann), 4, 7, 8, 10, 12, 14-15, 16, 18, 19
(photo: Iben Kaufmann), 21, 22-23, 24, 25, 26, 27 (photo: Kit Weiss), 28, 31,
32, 34, 36-37, 39, 40 (photo: Kit Weiss), 42, 44-45 (photo: Peter Nørby), 47,
48, 49, 50, 51, 52, 53 (photo: Jens Lindhe), 54, 56-57, 58 (photo: Kit Weiss):
The Royal Danish Collection, p. 11: The Royal Library, p. 55: The Museum of
National History, Frederiksborg Castle (photo: Ole Haupt).